GW01418184

# Talking of

# Pots,

# People &

# Points of View

*a new collection by*

*Alice Beer*

publisher: *poetry p f* — Nov 2005

# Acknowledgements

Magazines:

The Coffee House, Envoi, Poetry Monthly,
Reynard, The Rialto, Seam, Smiths Knoll,
Soundings, Time Haiku

Anthologies:

Barnet Poetry Competition, Beavering Around,
Dancing through the Pain, Exit 21, Poetry from
Leicestershire 1999, Pulling funny faces at the
Dog, Swarthmoor

## Thanks

Carole Satyamurti

Leicester Poetry Society and Soundswrite
Readings & Workshops, Huw Watkins,
Karin Koller, Pat Corina.

Almàssera Vella, the Arvon Foundation, the
Poetry School, Second Light, Smiths Knoll.


Previous collection:

*Facing Forward Looking Back*
Poetry Monthly Press, 1999,
ISBN: 1 903031 00 7



Cover Image: "Terracotta Sound" by Anne Stewart

publisher: *poetry p f*   — Nov 2005
www.poetrypf.co.uk
ISBN: 0-9552040-0-3 / 978-0-9552040-0-5

# Talking of Pots, People & Points of View

Alice Beer

Dedicated to Anne Stewart, my friend, who did so much more than publish this book.

My special thanks to:

Carole Satyamurti who kindly wrote the introduction to this book and for her exceptional quality of empathy, recognising what I wanted to say in my poems and helping me to find ways of doing so.

Leicester Poetry Society and Soundswrite Readings and Workshops, Huw Watkins, Karin Koller, Pat Corina and others helping me to attend and in other ways.

Also I have greatly benefited from the residential courses of the Almàssera Vella in Spain, the Arvon Foundation, Second Light, Smiths Knoll, the Poetry School and others in England and abroad.

I also thank my family and friends for all their help and patience.

Alice Beer,   November 2005

# Contents

# Contents (cont.)

# Contents (cont.)

# Introduction

The first time I met Alice Beer I was immediately struck by her openness to new ideas, and the enthusiasm with which she responded to suggestions, while at the same time having a very clear idea of what she wanted her work to achieve.

Her humour and kindness were very evident too. It may be thought that these are not necessarily poetic qualities but, in Alice's work, they are like a rich seam, running through poems of very diverse subject matter. Over the years, her work has gone from strength to strength. Her subject is the human condition, in the broadest sense. Whether in very personal poems, or in poems in which she imagines herself into the skin of literary characters, she writes with perceptiveness, compassion, courage and a humour that is never at other people's expense.

That she has lived for a very long time is a fact that is lightly worn. Her work is completely free of the nostalgia and narrow-minded tendency to judge others that beset many people in their later years, on the page and off it. Instead, she observes, and enjoys; and she writes wise poems in which she shares with us what she sees. Her language is direct and spare, like a window that allows us access into a different space without drawing attention to itself. It is language that is perfectly suited to serious purposes, as well as to wit, as in the delightful and accomplished haiku.

/...

The poems often evoke a feeling of 'just-rightness', as in the very moving ones that concern personal loss. Alice has a way of selecting images that seem unobtrusive, ordinary even, but which linger in the mind. I think this has something to do with their complete faithfulness to experience which, in her case, is more than a poetic strategy. It is an expression of integrity.

I am very pleased indeed that Alice Beer's poems will be reaching a wider audience, and know that they will be enjoyed by everyone who reads them.


**Carole Satyamurti**

### December 24th ●

Spellbound children watch
candle flames on the tree make
baubles, tinsel shine;

the room transformed, still—
until we raise our voices,
sing like every year

old and new carols
into the silent, wintery
night that is Christmas.


Tonight's full moon frowns
frostily on snow, shadows
stark on still white land.


The chilly sickle
of the waning moon above
the many-fingered
branches of leafless beech trees
heralds the unborn New Year.

● Publication: *Time Haiku*, Spring 2006. Included by kind
permission of the Editors, Erica Facey & Doreen King.

## Remembering Father

Mother had been restless all day
when you came home on leave
the year before the war ended.
The cape of your uniform
was wet through
and when you kissed me
drips from the peak of your cap
fell on my starched white apron.

## Questions and Answers

No one has found an answer to my question:
Where was my love before I met you?
It briefly showed its face
with Andrew and Sebastian
but only stayed with you and me.

And when you died, my love,
where did it go?
People will say:  it is still here,
you love him still.

I do, but it is just a memory
of mountain peaks, of glaciers
and dark pine forests
in the lake below.

## St. Valentine's Day

Seen from my window
slim middle aged man, under
his arm red roses

wrapped in indigo
paper, his face a broad smile;
anticipating.

For an instant his
smile makes me wish those six red
roses were for me.



St. Valentine the
saint, all but forgotten, yet
how we love his day.



## February Afternoon

Pastel blue sky, low
full moon behind bare branches
raised as in prayer.

## Love and the Bicycle

If you too had a bicycle
we could go out, the two of us
ride around the world together,
said he.

I've never had a bicycle.
I don't know how to ride one,
I can't afford to buy one,
said she.

I'll get a second hand one,
a really good and sturdy one,
I know the place to look for one,
said he.

He goes and buys a bicycle,
a really good and sturdy one.
It does not cost you much at all,
said he.

I don't know how to ride it,
I'm sure I'll never learn it,
I will fall off and hurt myself,
said she.

If I teach you to ride it,
you won't fall off and hurt yourself.
Will you come round the world with me?
he asked.

OK, she said
and smiled.

## How to Learn to Ride a Bicycle

Find a quiet spot without distractions.
Every little stone may prove an obstacle.
Ask a friend to help by holding the bicycle.
Sit on the seat and turn the pedals
with both your feet. The idea is
to keep your balance.

Don't look down at your feet, face forward.
Your friend will keep up with you.
Remember it is not as simple as it may look.
You will wobble, he will try to steady you.
Don't blame him if you fall; everybody does,
sooner or later.

It is easier than you think.
It is much harder than you think.
You depend on your friend, but don't
depend on him. Just bear in mind
it is his gift to you. If he has had enough
let him go.

## Weather Report

When first we met
the sun was blazing and the sky was blue
and clouds blew over the horizon
and rain swept over us
like a blessing.

And sun and rain and clouds and winds
continued their unending game
until it seemed to me
there were more clouds and rain
than sunshine, with the wind
growing cold

till snow came down
and a wall of ice
built up between us
that even the blazing sun
was not strong enough
to melt.


Chained to its vast bed,
stirred by storms and pulse of tides,
sings of drowned sailors.

## Before Sunrise

So still this early morning.
A band of greeny light
where earth meets sky.

One cloud lying behind
the firs and hawthorn;
above, the blue grey sky
as yet untouched by the unrisen sun.

And as I pass the window
shadowy shapes
of two bats winging their way
back to their roosts and rest.


## The Fields in Spring

In ploughed fields the hare
wakes, sits up, sniffs cool spring air,
streaks back to its form.

Hawthorn round the field
bursts into white blossoms.
I think of last year, when

we strolled along those
fields, you and I, smelling dark
brown earth, young green wheat....

## March

Resting on a seat
on New Walk, I see many
people passing by,

watch the sunshine bring
out their incipient smile, see
it spread from their lips

all over their face, reach
me, including me in their
joy of nascent spring.

## A Wedding Tanka
*( for Emma and Paul )*

Congratulations
on your wedding.  May you make
each other happy
and your love prove strong to the
end of your time and beyond.

### 3 Haiku about Quakers

*for an exhibition in Leicester Meeting House*

Who are these Quakers?
Folk like you and me, searching
for God inside us.

People who believe
that there is something of God
in everybody.

People like yourself,
who listen in silence for
the presence of God.

## The Elsinore Diaries:

*"Imagine that Fortinbras, finding these*
*after the events, had hidden them in a secret place..."*

Elizabeth S.C. Brandow

## I    Claudius' Diary: Decision

Second by birth and second ever since;
I've had enough. My mind's made up.
I won't be playing second fiddle all my life.

And Gertrude, now mature, still young,
has lost none of her charms.
To think of her sharing my Brother's bed—
no, not much longer.

## II  Claudius' Diary: A few Days after the Murder

It was quite easy, in the end.
Nobody there to watch me,
it was a moment's work.
And he disfigured, looking so repulsive
she could not bring herself to touch him.
I hope her memory of him is spoiled for ever.

I managed to put on a great performance
as his brother, so full of anguish, sorrow,
my one desire to help him, ease his pain,
comfort the grieving widow, assist in any way
I could devise to make her feel dependent on me.

I bide my time, but in due course
I will declare to her my passion.
Also her duty to the nation.
The people need a King.

### III Queen Gertrude's Diary: The King's Death

So quick it seemed unreal was his death.
A serpent bit him as he rested in the orchard.
He could not even say his prayers,
repent his sins, receive Holy Communion
that would allow his soul to rise to Heaven.

And to my shame I must confess,
despite his pleading eyes,
I could no more caress his face, always so smooth,
now blistered with some horrid, leprous rash
than touch a slimy, wart-encrusted toad
or writhing worms.

I mourned him, yes, I loved and mourned my King
and I am grateful to his brother Claudius.
He is my comfort, my support and I love him,
can not deny his wish to marry me,
barely a month after the funeral.
And so be it.

## IV  Queen Gertrude's Diary: A Week after the Wedding

Quite suddenly I woke, hearing his voice
as if he lay beside me, not his brother.
"Gertrude," he said, calling me: "Gertrude."
I felt as if an icy hand had touched me.
"Where are you?" I asked softly, not wishing
to disturb my husband, my new husband.
There was no answer but the curtain blew.
I lay awake a long time, wondering,
listening to the storm.

## V   Queen Gertrude's Diary: Some Time after the Wedding

Bleak widowhood was not for me.
I freely gave my love to Claudius
who is so different, so full of fire
in his passion for me.
Formerly bitter, sullen, harsh,
married to me he seems at ease.

Not so dear Hamlet.
He bears a grudge against his uncle
who tries so hard to win his confidence.
Hamlet abhors our marriage,
blames me for what he calls unseemly haste,
my lack of chastity and dignity
supplanting him whom he had loved and honoured.

In fact I think his jealousy
has made him downright rude.
I am afraid the King
will lose his patience any day,
talks about meaning not to tolerate
Hamlet's behaviour any longer.
And what am I to do then?
He is my son, but there are limits.

## VI Hamlet's Diary: Immediately after Seeing his Father's Ghost

I wish I'd never seen his ghostly figure,
so similar to what he'd been and yet transformed.
I thought at first it could have been
a figment of my imagination, but no.

The words he spoke, the manner of his speech,
the tale he told me so convincing,
so horrible beyond belief.
And yet it is in keeping
with the nature of my uncle
who now usurps his place.
He is a man without a conscience,
capable of the worst misdeeds.

And I alone charged with
the vengeance of this murder.
What can I do against this
evil, cunning man, all on my own?

It's madness to attempt it but I must
if it's the last thing that I do.

## VII   Queen Gertrude's Diary: The Change in Hamlet

Thinking of Hamlet, I remember him
just as he used to be.
How he became so changed I cannot fathom.

He who was spirited but never ruthless
ventures wild phrases, threatening speeches,
exaggerated gestures, speaks words altered in meaning.
I love my son, thought him perfection.
Now I don't know him any more.

The good Polonius tells me that Ophelia,
whom Hamlet courted for a while,
on his advice withdrew her favours.
Now he was wondering if this
has robbed him of his balance.

I'm not so sure.  I know he is upset
about his Father's sudden death,
also my marriage.
But it is irritating beyond measure.
Consider my position,
the Queen, the Mother of a mad man!

### VIII Hamlet's Diary: A Few Days after Seeing his Father's Ghost

This one encounter with my Father's ghost
has changed my life completely.
After a sleepless night
the consequences rise
like sheer grey cliffs
out of the ever restless sea.

I can not meet my Mother's eyes.
I must confront her with the facts
as I now know them,
can be her son no longer
until I've shared the truth with her
and she forsakes her marriage
with her husband's murderer.

Farewell the pleasant banter with my friends,
farewell my fair Ophelia,
farewell for ever to my carefree youth.

## IX  Queen Gertrude's Diary: The Players

The players came to our court today,
it is not often that we get a chance.
I always liked them, they are skilful.
They usually give a good performance.

This time the play was not so good,
we did not stay to see the end.
Their Queen talked on and on about her love,
how she would always venerate the King's memory—
who'd said that he was ailing—
would never love another man at any time,
no matter how many years would pass.
No woman in her middle years should say that
when she feels capable of passion.

And then the nephew slays the King
by pouring poison in his ear
while he lies sleeping.
At seeing this, Claudius calls for lights
and leaves, most of us with him.

He was livid, I've never seen him like this.
What sort of play is this?
It was not entertaining as it should.
Villainous fantasy, he called it.
So far removed from real life.

## X    Claudius' Diary: After the Death of Polonius

I'm sorry for the good Polonius,
a true and faithful servant,
although he never spoke one word
when three or four would do.
He can be spared —
did me the greatest service by his death.

And as for Hamlet:
this rash deed seals his fate.
He has to leave the court at once.
His doting Mother can't refuse.

With Rosenkranz and Guildenstern
he must depart for England now.
I will brook no delay.
The ship is waiting
and the letters written.

## In the Garden

When she was nearly eleven years old—
a rather delicate girl, perhaps a little
given to reading too many stories and playing
on her own—she became very ill.  Her body
grew so hot that she left her bed
and went far away into a cool garden.

There the sun threw a golden light on everything.
Each green leaf, every blade of grass
breathed freshness and fragrance into the clear air.
The flowers shone in rich glowing colours
and birds sang as she had never heard them
sing before.  She felt a lot better straight away.
There was no one else about, yet
she did not feel lonely, just at peace.
She wished she could stay there forever.

But she had to return and though she tried hard
to find the way back, all she was left with
were dreams and a strange longing she could not
understand.  But somehow she knew the time would come
when the way would remain hidden no longer.

## My Angel

The first time that I saw him
was on the day I started school.
I knew I had a Guardian Angel,
my Mother often mentioned him
when I had only grazed my knees
and once at a bad fall
that nearly broke my skull.

I did not actually see him then,
I felt him take my free hand—
my Mother held the other—and I thought
there was a sort of shimmering
where adults have their shoulders.
It was so comforting. I knew
I'd be all right when she had gone.

And once when seriously ill, my body
feverish, hurting, restless,
when all I wanted was to be free of it,
he laid cool hands on my hot forehead,
murmuring soothing words I did not understand.
But sleep came and a better morning.

He takes the shape of ordinary people:
the nurse who brought me cooling drinks
the friend, unburdening herself,
allowing insight into my own problems,
that woman on the bus who
with her friendly words to me, a stranger,
gave me the confidence to carry on.

/...

These days I don't see much of him—
perhaps he knows there is no special need.
But I believe I will perceive him
as he is, next time he comes.

**So You Want to be a Potter?**

Here are some rules:
nose above the centre of the wheel
to find the centre of your pot.
The wholeness of your pot
depends on being centred.

Shape your pot from the inside.
It's not what people see
but it's what matters.
Once you have got it right inside
the rest sees to itself.  Well, more or less.

Balance your hands, make them a team,
one inside, one outside your pot.
While one hand pushes up,
the other gives support,
one as important as the other.

And keep a steady pace,
although your speed must vary.
There should be nothing sudden
to upset the growth.
I wish you joy!

## What I learned in my pottery class

That this lump of clay on your wheel
behaves like a living being.

That it needs to be centred and
you have to assert your control over it.

That it responds to a little, gentle
swearing, —uttered under your breath—
but more explicit Anglo-Saxon words
have the opposite effect.

That your teacher can give you sound advice
and you better listen.

That effort is not always rewarded.

That off the wheel a small bit of clay
goes a long way.

That a little cheating is allowed
but don't bank on its success.

That sheer strength counts
though it is not all that's required.

That in Pottery round is beautiful;
in exceptional cases however, like love, etc,
beauty is in the eyes of the beholder.

## What I learned living on my own again

That grieving is natural and hurts.

That it is easy to forget
one's children of any age
also have to come to terms with their loss.

That it is important to fill
the space left empty.

That Christmas and Birthdays are best
spent with family or friends.

That "alone" is not synonymous with "lonely".

That even your friends prefer to share good times
with you rather than your grief.

That it is possible to go out on one's own.

That it is easier to get to know strangers
when not part of a couple.

That one can still laugh and enjoy oneself.

That one person might be able to do things
that were too expensive for two but

that a bargain is not a bargain
when one can use only half of it.

/...

That one can indulge one's own taste.

That freedom is something to treasure.

That life is still worth living.

## Statement

When Helen sits on a seat
looking at the world around her
it does not mean she is idle,
just busy practising
being an old woman.

She had to learn to admit
that she quickly gets breathless
and is not as strong
as in her earlier years.

So she gladly accepts help
cheerfully offered by younger people
without feeling smothered,
patronized, looked down on.

Acknowledging
that her physical radius has shrunk,
she can watch them without envy,
doing what she used to.

She regrets her limitations
but they have not made her bitter.
She still has a full life
because for years now
she has been practising
to be an old woman.

## You and I •

are one.
We've been together
since before my birth.
It's wrong to talk as if
you and I
were just two different entities.
Each one of us
has many parts
working in harmony
most of the time.

You and I
faithfully served each other,
looked after each other
most of the time.
Sometimes you have rebelled against me
and I, at times, have found you cumbersome.

You and I
have undergone many changes
yet we are still the same.

You and I
will stay together
till death will part us.
What happens to the I
I cannot tell;
you may be useful after that,
there is no real waste.

• Publication: *Envoi*, Issue 143. Included by kind permission of
the Editor, Roger Elkin

## Seven Shapes of Silence    •

The concentrated silence
of my cat, Blossom,
meticulously
licking her paws
before washing herself and

her stealthy silence
when pouncing on a bird
or a mouse.

The heavy silence
when a brewing storm
takes a breath
before breaking.

The impartial silence
of the empty wardrobe
in a hotel room.

The expectant silence
of a Quaker meeting,
just breathing.

The brooding silence
of a turned-off fountain,
bereft of purpose.

/...

My own awed silence
when my first pregnancy
was confirmed
in September 1939.

* Publication: *Envoi*, Issue 143. Included by kind permission of
the Editor, Roger Elkin

## Poetry Courses

Every course is different.

The success of the course depends on the students
as much as the tutors.

The most famous poet is not necessarily the best tutor.

Tutors are human.

The course works better if the tutors come prepared.

Tutors can not be prepared for every eventuality.

Your contribution to the course makes a difference.

Listening can be as great a contribution as speaking.

Your expectation of the course is important.

The course can be very different from your expectation.

You can't expect every participant to contribute
something of importance to you.

Anybody's contribution, however apparently trivial,
may be just what another person needs to hear.

/...

Poetry is not something that can be taught.

There are many things you can learn about poetry.

## Poetry Workshop

Why does it seem much
easier to judge your colleagues'
poems than your own?

Why does the one you
value the highest get the
thumbs down by your friends?

And one that might just
make the grade, get the applause?
I wish I could tell.
And still we bring our poems
week by week to judge, be judged.

## Islands

Greeks call Corfu a
garden island set in the
blue Ionian sea.

There Casa Lucia
feels like a fresh green island
amidst olive groves.

Swallows dip in its
pool, an island set among
cool jasmine arbours.


## Oranges

Globes of sunshine from
southern lands, Spain, Greece—each one
echoing the sun.




It takes time to make
friends; it takes no time at all
to make enemies.

## Journey and Arrival

After the train and the boat,
another train from Dover.
Ambling through the Kent fields,
past farms and oasthouses,
the vast strings of houses,
pocket handkerchief gardens.
We thought: This is England.

In a taxi, shepherded by a woman from the YWCA
from Victoria to St. Pancras.
After seemingly endless London
small towns along the route,
sheep in the countryside,
hedges in bloom.
We thought: This is England.

Collected from the station by our employers,
a car ride past fruit trees covered in bloom —
in Austria blossom time was over.
We felt: This is England.

Shown to our room, two iron bedsteads,
one chest of drawers, a shabby wardrobe,
no heating,
told to be down in the kitchen
at quarter to seven next morning.
Anna and I exchanged glances,
thought: So, this is England.

## Baker Street Station

Pigeons think it's theirs.
They generously allow trains
and humans its use.

## Time and Motion
### (a found poem)

This train goes to London St Pancras
Calling at
Long Eaton Loughborough Leicester Luton St Pancras

This train goes to London St Pancras
Calling at
Loughborough Leicester Luton St Pancras

This train goes to London St Pancras
Calling at
Leicester Luton St Pancras

This train goes to London St Pancras
Calling at
Luton St Pancras

This train goes to London St Pancras

Luxury flats where
gardens used to be. Sparrows
grow scarce in our town.


## To Aldermaston—by Coach

So there we were, going to Aldermaston
along the familiar roads, as spring
was clothing trees and hedgerows
in the first, deceptively tender-looking
leaves and blossoms, not marching
but to witness the marchers.

They kept us waiting.  When at last they came,
weary and footsore—some of them, at least—
we gave them such a welcome as if
they had been gone for months, not days.
And we could see their backs straighten
and their worn faces smiling
at their achievement and tears
form in their eyes while mine
were overflowing as I stood
at the fence, waving and clapping...

## Coach Tour to the Lakes

### Staffordshire Moors Village

Windswept houses crowd
round old church, its square tower
low for protection.

### Lancashire Village

Top of the hill — church,
down by the river — mill, linked
by straggling Main Street.

### Between Kendal and Penrith

White mist — a cloak thrown
over the land about us.
Fells, lakes all vanished.

### Penrith to Keswick

Distant ash trees spread
skeletal branches like fans
against cloudless sky.

Becks etched deeply in
steep fell sides, like scratch marks by
prehistoric beasts.

Near Keswick, 9.3.2003

Mare and foal grazing
unaware of human cares,
growing threat of war.

Rare March lambs playing,
head butting, watched by their dam—
crazy as March hares.


Bowness, Lake Windermere

Sun, blue sky, white clouds,
white sails on choppy water,
reeds shield black moor hens.

## Walking Home

Do you remember
after all those years
the evening you walked me home
because my boyfriend
had to finish work for his course?
And the street lights reflected,
all shiny and distorted in the puddles
the rain had left?

Do you remember feeling, like me,
we should see more of each other
and how my boyfriend became
just one of the crowd—
how we met again and again
and then went away together
on my birthday?

I do not think you do
wherever you are now,
after all those years.
Or do the dead remember
like the living?

## Fever

I became ill while you were overseas
and I longed for you to stroke
my aching head and body,
take away the pain in my throat
when I heard the fox's eery call
at the bottom of the garden
and suddenly I was there,
hunted by packs of hounds
their red tongues hanging out,
dripping, ears laid back,
the galloping horses' hooves
in time with my racing pulse
while I was looking for you
under hedges and piles of rubble
in the streets after the bombings
and I felt so helpless I started to cry
when the nurse woke me...

## This Morning

we were there, in our walled back garden,
and you, my love, picked a few Coxes off the tree
which puzzled me because we never had an apple tree
and even as I thought this you were gone, so I
went through the back door into the kitchen
with its red quarry-tiled floor and
the blue and white check curtains, the sink
under the window, the saucepans upside down
on the shelf opposite, the mug tree
with its blue and white mugs on the cupboard
next to the draining board as usual so I wondered
what the young man, reminding me of you
was doing in my kitchen with his arms
round a laughing young woman, when I woke
and remembered it was more than 18 years
since I moved to my sunny little flat
overlooking the square.

## One Little Star

When the brittle, little star
falls from the sky
and lies on the pavement
the girl picks it up,
wraps it in a tissue and
puts it in her pocket.

Lovingly she mends all the cracks.
At night it fills her room
with its silvery light.
She dreams she walks along the river
hand in hand with her boyfriend,
the moon, three quarters full,
mirrored in the flowing water,
a thin glittering triangle.

In the morning the little star's light
is spent. She hides it in a drawer
with her coral necklace, her silver
charm bracelet. She never tells anybody
about it; her friends can't understand
why nowadays they think of stars
and moonlight when they see her.

POWER

POWER

POWER

POWER

POWER

A field in Somerset,
power lines stretching into the horizon
and underneath
the artist has planted rows and rows
of fluorescent tubes, upright like tulips,
white mostly, some in colours.

Striking, particularly when you notice
these tubes glow with light.
No wires to connect them,
no switches.

The artist states it is not his intention
to prove creation of electric fields
beneath the pylons, nor that they cause
clusters of illness, cancers.

Interpretation lies with us.
"The Sorcerer's Apprentice" comes to mind.

## Comments

"Count your blessings" you
say. I do, but I have learned
not to count on them.


A smile often works
as a switch for the one light
deep within us all.


You must strike a match
before your candle's light can
dispel the darkness.


"I'm wasted." No one,
nobody, nothing is lost,
only recycled.


Like priceless pearls or
worthless beads, days follow days
on a thread called life.


Raindrops: crystals, pearls
on rose petals, leaves, sweet peas—
oceans in each drop.

## Casa Lucia

The pine tree in the middle of the lawn
seems to have grown too tall and so
they cut the main trunk off;
the other branches now
are arms stretched up to heaven.

They have grown taller than the tree had ever been—
children often grow taller than their parents
but they don't wait until their elders have departed.
These usurp the space given before
to older branches taking up the light.

The pine tree and the bushes forming half a circle
around the lawn are one; one also with the gardens
skirting the different houses.  Their harmony
embraces us into the one-ness
with the people, dogs and cats,
the dusky green of olive trees,
the smell of jasmine in the arbour,
the tantalising apricots, too hard to eat,
the swallows dipping in the pool,
the fireflies at night,
the sickle of the moon.

## How to demonstrate facts or a principle •

With a pencil
make 2 dots on a piece of paper
one above the other, some distance apart.

Join them by a straight line.
This is your statement.

At about the middle of the distance
put another point just a fraction
of a millimetre to the right.

Draw a new line through these three points,
nobody will see any difference.

Repeat this process several times.
Your line now will show
a small but definable divergence
from the original one.

If anyone notices, explain
it is seen from a different angle
or a new perspective.

You can repeat this process
indefinitely.
Call it Politics.

• Publication: *Envoi*, Issue 143. Included by kind permission of the
Editor, Roger Elkin

## Pride & Prejudice
## Some of Jane Austen's Characters Speak

### Mr Bennet Sums Up

The way life shaped itself is disappointing.
I know I am not blameless.  Not that I seem
to have much to complain of, a good house
and land, left me by my parents,
enough to live on in good style—
though nothing for the future of my family.
My two eldest are a pleasure to be with,
the other three, each in their own way—
nothing but worry, useless.

What could I say about my wife?
I fell in love with her, a pretty face,
good at dancing, quick repartees
which I mistook for wit.  Only in time
I learned how much I was mistaken.

I vainly tried to widen her horizons
beyond marrying off our daughters and gossip.
And with the flight of youth her temper
has grown worse.  She takes refuge
in "her nerves" and I, instead of trying
to appease her, retire to my library.

Talking to her has grown into a chore.
I am polite in front of servants,
that is the measure of my care for her.

/...

The older girls, Jane and Elizabeth,
have never let me down. The others fill me
with despair. Their Mother was never able
to control them. When we go out, they shame me
with their wild behaviour, showing off.
I shrug my shoulders and make fun of them.
I know I should have shown more interest,
exerted influence on their education.
But what's the use? I hope my daughters
will show more wisdom in their choice!


## Mrs Bennet Remonstrates

Their Father has forgotten
he married me for love. Jane's beauty
and her sister's good looks have come
from me. And I was pretty lively,
could hold my own in any company.
Some officers would have been glad
to marry me. He offered first.

Five daughters later, my looks
are not quite what they were. Still
I compare well with our neighbours.
But he has changed, sits in his library
all day when he's not shooting pheasants.
He shows me no respect, pays no attention
to my wishes, never consults me.
No wonder my nerves are in shreds.

/...

The Lady Lucas and my sister Phillips
understand me, although their husbands
have proved much better than my own.
And that entail! I've told him many times
to do something about it.
But he takes no notice, as usual.

Jane's very helpful too when I am feeling low —
I wish her sisters were the same!
Elizabeth is merely polite to me, Mary
can think only of her books and my dear Lydia
and Kitty of officers and dances.
Their Father finds much to criticise,
forgets his youth when he was not averse
to entertainment. For my part, I'm sure
I do my best.


### Mary Bennet Explains

Jane is the beauty of the family,
Lizzie very pretty and a wit,
Mother's pet Lydia loud, wilful, ignorant —
she can't and won't restrain her —
and Kitty follows in her wake.

I am the brainy one.
I will impress with my accomplishments.
While Jane and Lizzie stitch at their embroidery
and Lydia and Kitty moan or giggle,
I'm hard at work to master
the most improving library books,
practice difficult phrases on our pianoforte.

/...

The others just don't understand me,
say I'm righteousness personified.
They laugh behind my back.
I do not care as long as I am following
the right path, helping them cultivate
their minds. And what is wrong with that?


### Charlotte Lucas Considers

Elizabeth tries to hide her disappointment,
she thinks I'm throwing myself away
by marrying this foolish, self-opinionated man.

But looked at rationally
what choice do I have?
I am not pretty like her
and without her wit.
We have no money, I am twenty seven.
Am I to stay at home, the daughter
of a vain semi-gentleman, my Gossip Mother,
and all my sisters gradually starting
to wear their skirts long, their hair up?

I have no feelings for him,
find his company irksome but
one can get used to anything.
I'll keep him busy in the garden
and working at his sermons.
A bit of flattery will soon satisfy
his vanity, sense of his own importance
and I shall be quite comfortable.

/...

Practical, that's what I have to be
by choice if not by inclination.
As "parson's wife" I'll have respectability,
my own house, servants.

And as to Lady Catherine de Bourgh:
apparently deferring to her wishes
won't be so hard, neither will conversation
as she herself does all the talking.
I'm sure I do the right thing
in the circumstances.


### Elizabeth Bennet about her Sister Jane

Jane, dear Jane, what can I say about her?
Sometimes I think it is not fair
that so much beauty and such goodness
have been conferred on just one person.

I love her dearly, who could do otherwise?
And yet, I must confess I get impatient with her.
Setting herself the highest standards of behaviour
makes her not blind to other people's failings;
she always tries, however, to provide a reason,
an excuse for their mistakes, weaknesses.

I could not find the tolerance for our Mother's
outbursts; when thwarted she will rail against
injustice, being wronged as always, take to her room,
incapable of facing her allotted tasks.  Jane
tries hard to help her back to contentment.

/...

Jane is not one to talk about her feelings;
when all goes well with her she radiates happiness.
I saw her growing pale and quiet when family
and friends of the man she loved, spirited
him away, regarding her connections not acceptable;
she suffered silently, whilst I would rage
against such fate, see meanness, treachery,
betrayal and probably not be mistaken.

Well, in the end misunderstandings were cleared up.
It is a joy to see her blossoming again,
I revel in her beauty, her happiness restored.


### Mr Bingley about Mr Darcy

We have been friends for years.  I expect
he likes my easy-going temperament, my relaxed ways.
He is somewhat older and much more serious.
I feel honoured by his friendship.

Darcy, a man of rank and fortune like his Father
before him, takes his responsibilities
seriously.  Pemberley and the land around it,
the welfare of his tenants are in his charge.
He is a just and caring landlord.

He is demanding of himself and others.
He does not compromise his duties,
requires the same of his friends, detests
pretentiousness, lies, neglect;  he feels contempt
for all that thus offend.  I admire him for it.

/...

An only child till he was ten, he never had to share
his rocking-horse, his toys with others
nor knew the squabbles of the nursery; I had
an older and a younger sister. He never
learned one can fight bitterly one moment,
be friends again the next.

What he lacks is ease. Tall, with good features
he is much in demand at social functions, dances.
His sensibility makes him reluctant
to mix with people outside the circle
of his family and friends. No wonder
he has the reputation of being proud.

Just once in our years of friendship
trust in his judgement led me to make
a big mistake. When he confessed his error
it made me very angry. Humble in his remorse
he did his best to help make it undone.
I have forgiven him. We are still friends.

## Talking about Clichés

words or phrases
that will express a subject
succinctly and
without doubt
so well
that
any Tom, Dick and Harry
can use it to advantage
but which
proper poets
must
avoid like the plague
scratch their heads
rack their brains
go to any length
to try and find
a substitute
that nearly
hits the nail on the head
lest they be branded
as being
trivial
lazy
commonplace
beyond the pale
lacking in originality
in their writing
walking the well trodden path
and
taking the easy way
out.

### Literature
with abject apologies to Hilaire Belloc.

Emilia Smith from  Birkenhead
insisted that her daily bread
would have to come not through her looks
but through her writing many books,

sat all her days and half the night
with not a thought about her sight
and scribble, scribble went her pen
as she sat in her little den

and covered papers, sheet on sheet,
with writing, orderly and neat
which she sent off—and very soon
she was engaged by Mills and Boon.

Her Mother warned her: No girl should—
as all this writing surely would—
damage her eyes, have to wear glasses,
as no man ever would make passes.

But she pooh-poohed this strange idea
of radiant beauty—was that clear?—
she'd never marry, make her name
striding through the portals of fame.

Stranger than fiction was her fate,
at Mills and Boon she met her mate
and both went on to gather prizes
of ever increasing worth and sizes,

/...

writing of youngsters, straights and gays,
in long lines, bristling with clichés
that caught the hearts of young and old,
the timid, struggling and the bold.

Their union, tender, full of love
produced more books and other stuff
and to her Mother's pride and joy
three pretty girls, one bouncing boy.

## Willendorf Venus •

My man showed me the stone he'd carved,
said it was me. It had my curls
but was not like the women I know.

I have big breasts, fed my ten children,
but these boobs were enormous,
also the hips and stomach
and the labia,
curved as my lips.

If I could carve a stone I'd make a man.
He would be tall and strong
just like my man.

I'd give him hands and arms for bow and arrows
to kill the wild black boar and the red deer,
and make him a big penis, long as his arms,
to give me ten more children.

• The Willendorf Venus: an archaeological find in a remote
valley in the Austrian Alps, 4 inches high, estimated about 25000
years old.

### Not a New Man

When thinking of the state of our marriage
I fear the minusses outweigh the plusses.
I really consider that you've spoilt the children.

Their table manners are atrocious. My Mother,
I am afraid, does not approve of swearing
and they don't seem to do much homework.

Words fail me to describe your cooking and
tidiness or economy are not your forte,
but I admit you are superb in bed.

## After the Creation

When God had finished creating
the earth and the sea and the heavens
and every living thing that swam in the water
and flew in the air
and dwelt on the land—

when he had made man in his image,
male and female,
he felt exceedingly happy.
A smile spread over his face
that lit up the earth and the firmament
with the joy of creation.

And to single out his favourite—
man made in his image—
he bestowed on him the gift
of creativity.

Reflecting on it afterwards he wondered
if —man being man—
he had not been a little impetuous.

## First Meeting

Nothing special about that evening, lots of people there
and one person I had not seen before

and nothing special about the room in the old house
in the centre of town, where we used to meet

and I noticed him, slightly older than me, his lower lip
more prominent, and an expression of puzzling dissatisfaction.

There were posters along the wall, about equality, unity,
the horrors of war, possibility of peaceful coexistence.

Nothing special about me having forgotten my book
and him offering to share his with me

and nothing special about me, not very tall or slim
and I did not think my glasses helped my appearance

and our host's cat Milly came into the room, meowed
and rubbed itself against my legs and my chair

and my boyfriend took his handkerchief out of his pocket,
cleaned his glasses and then rubbed it all over his face

and outside, under the streetlights, the rain came down,
washing the dust off the roads, so they looked freshly cleaned

and every drop made shining rings in the puddles, cutting
into each other and making the pavement seem alive.

## Intruder

I wake just before five.
It is still dark—turn on the light,
go to the bathroom. On the way
I notice something brown next to the sink.

Ugh! A surprising mixture
of disgust, fear, and indignation rises.
What is it doing in my territory?
Let it go back where it belongs!

Five minutes later I look at it again.
It is not slimy, not even ugly,
its milk-chocolately body covered
by skin with regular parallel ridges,

the front third lifted up; I feel—
although I can detect no features—
it's giving me a friendly, tentative grin
beneath those horns. This is imagination
gone too far.

Disgust has gone. Nevertheless
as I go back to bed, I have made up my mind:
tonight I must make sure
the plug sits firmly in its hole.

When I get up at seven, it has gone.

## The Present

After the birthday party the rocket lamp
sits on the table and I switch it on.
At first there is no change,
then blisters form in the red wax
that elongate, break into bubbles, rise,
stir memories of air expelled
by dolphins breathing out.

Sometimes they merge on top
but mostly they float down,
slide past their rising siblings,
regain their shape, descend to the bottom,
are carried up again.

I watch them, mesmerised, till I
find my attention wandering.
Once more I press the switch
and wonder, suddenly, who
is operating mine.

Four chairs, music stands.
The empty hall still breathing
Mozart, Beethoven.


My black puppy's tail
wagging like a metronome
at the tempo of
allegro vivace as
she brings back the rubber bone.


### Rowan Tree in November

Birds took the berries,
storms spread its golden-red leaves
all over our lawn

## Visitor

Dusk had set in as I went down the paddock
to shut the hen house and noticed
a funny kind of dog moving away.  Up at the house
the people laughed at me:  haven't you ever seen
a fox?  I had to answer:  No, there were
no foxes in Vienna where I had lived.

Many years later I saw this creature of the dark
again, in our Square, on grass but underneath
the street lamp, as cool as anything;  it just
stood there before it vanished, blending into the hedge.

After that, whenever I woke up, I looked for it
but never saw it until the other morning
while it was still dark.  The spotlight on the statue
half lit the Square as it stood under the leafless sycamore,
head lowered, watching something I could not see.

But when my kitchen light came on it trotted off,
not leisurely and not in a hurry, intent
on its own business and left me wondering
why I felt as if the clouds had lifted
on this dark December morning.

## On Growing Old

Like mice in the night
the years that pass are gnawing
at our life ahead.

Bit by bit the paths
our life takes seem narrower,
steeper and more rugged.

The ruts get deeper,
the woods more dense, the bright star
before us brighter.